ELEVATOR PLUS

ELEVATOR PLUS

SUMEET KATARIYA

Available on amazonkindle

Worldwide Published by

Pendown Press

PREMIUM BUSINESS PUBLISHER

PENDOWN PRESS LLP
An ISO 9001 & ISO 14001 Certified Co.,
Regd. Office: 3767A, Kanhaiya Nagar,
Tri Nagar, Delhi-110035
Ph.: 8130886000, 9650072927
E-mail: info@pendownpress.com
Branch Office: 1A/2A, 20, Hari Sadan, Ansari Road,
Daryaganj, New Delhi-110002
Ph.: 011-45794768
Website: PendownPress.com

Edition: 2026
Price: ₹ 299
ISBN: 978-93-6338-999-1

Layout and Cover Designed by Pendown Graphics Team

DEDICATED TO EVERYONE
WHO KEEPS THE ELEVATOR
INDUSTRY MOVING QUIETLY,
EVERY SINGLE DAY.

Table of Contents

Foreword

A fundamental requirement for any successful business is robust operations anchored in process discipline. Whether a company is small and aspiring to grow, or large and working to sustain itself, operations remain the backbone. This becomes even more critical in industries such as healthcare, aviation, and vertical transportation, where operational discipline and safety are inseparable.

The elevator industry, unlike many businesses that operate within controlled environments, is deeply dependent on field operations. Historically, leadership decisions within the global elevator industry were driven by professionals with strong hands-on operational experience, particularly field experience. There was a clear understanding that operations could either strengthen or dismantle a company. This belief shaped the industry for the first two decades of my nearly four decades in vertical transportation.

Over the last two decades, however, a noticeable shift has occurred. General management skills have increasingly taken precedence over hands-on operational leadership. Field experience has gradually moved to the background, while processes have become more commercially oriented. At the same time, the rise of business automation encouraged elevator companies to adopt digital systems to manage scale and complexity.

While automation brought efficiency, it also introduced a critical flaw. Most enterprise automation platforms placed finance at the centre, forcing operations and reporting to adapt to financial structures rather than reflecting the realities of elevator field operations. As a result, operations, meant to support growth, began to weaken. In many cases, this slowed progress; in others, it destabilised entire organisations.

When leadership lacks practical field understanding, this deterioration can accelerate quickly. Several once-dominant companies across industries stand as evidence of what happens when operational fundamentals are neglected. This is not to diminish the importance of commercial discipline, but to reinforce a simple truth: long-term commercial success cannot exist without strong operational foundations.

What makes this book particularly relevant is Sumeet Katariya's clear understanding of this imbalance. He has analysed the divide between commercial systems and operational realities with rare depth and clarity. This book presents his perspective on restoring that balance. It offers elevator industry leaders a comprehensive view of operational efficiency, rooted in field realities, yet aligned with modern automation and data intelligence.

More importantly, it challenges the industry to return to its operational core, without resisting progress. It calls for discipline, structure, and clarity within the context of a fast-moving, technology-driven world.

For those responsible for building, running, and sustaining elevator businesses, this book is not just timely; it is necessary.

~Tak Mathews

About Tak Mathews

Tak Mathews brings nearly four decades of experience in the construction and vertical transportation industry. He is the Principal Consultant at TAK Consulting and a recognised authority on elevator safety, standards, and operational governance.

He serves as a representative on the Lifts and Escalators Standards Committee of the Bureau of Indian Standards (BIS) and is the Chairman of the Lifts and Escalators Section of the National Building Code of India. He is also the Founder of the Elevator & Escalator Safety Trust (EEST), India, an organisation dedicated to improving safety standards and awareness in the industry.

Mr. Mathews holds an engineering degree from the University of Dar es Salaam (Tanzania), an MBA from the Birla Institute of Technology, Mesra (India), and is an alumnus of IMD, Lausanne (Switzerland). He is a Chartered Engineer and continues to contribute actively to shaping industry standards and best practices.

Preface

Why This Book Matters to the Elevator Industry

This book was written with one simple thought in mind.
To speak honestly with people who run elevator businesses.

Not as an expert speaking down.
Not as a teacher giving lessons.
But as someone who understands how this business feels on a daily basis.

Running an elevator business is not easy. It demands attention every day. There is always something to handle, someone to answer, and some responsibility that cannot be ignored. Many times, you keep going without stopping to ask whether the business is serving you, or you are only serving the business.

This book is not about telling you what you are doing wrong.
It is not about comparing you with others.
And it is not about showing how things should be done.

It is about giving you a moment to pause.

A moment to step back and look at your business without urgency.
A moment to think without pressure.
A moment to reflect without judgement.

You do not need special education to read this book.
You do not need technical knowledge.
You only need your own experience and honesty.

Every page is written in simple language, keeping real people in mind. People who work hard, carry responsibility, and still try to build something meaningful for their families and teams.

If at any point while reading, you feel that the words sound familiar, that is intentional. This book does not come from theory. It comes from lived realities.

Take your time with it. Read it slowly. There is no rush.

If by the end, you feel a little clearer about your business, or even about yourself, then this book has served its purpose.

Thank you for being here.

Acknowledgements

This book would not have been possible without the people who stood by me throughout this journey. Many of them may not appear on these pages, but their support is felt in every line.

To My Parents

You have always believed in me, even during times when the path was unclear. Your values, guidance, and quiet strength have shaped who I am today. Everything I build carries your influence.

To My Wife, Sanjiwani

You have been my constant support through every phase. You manage our home and office with care and patience while allowing me the space to focus on my vision. Your understanding and calm presence mean more to me than words can express.

To My Son, Anvit

You bring joy and meaning to my life every day. Your laughter, curiosity, and innocence remind me why balance, honesty, and kindness matter. You inspire me to keep growing, not just as a professional, but as a person.

To My Coach and Mentor

Your guidance helped me see situations clearly when I felt unsure. Thank you for sharing your experience, asking the right questions, and encouraging me to move forward with confidence.

To My Team at Accucia

This journey would not be possible without your hard work and commitment. Thank you for turning ideas into reality and for building systems that help elevator businesses work better and grow steadily.

To the Early Users and Supporters of ElevatorPlus

Your trust gave this idea its first real direction. Thank you for believing in ElevatorPlus at a time when it was still taking shape. Your confidence and feedback played a key role in turning an idea into something meaningful.

To Elevator Business Owners Around the World

Thank you to the elevator business owners across the globe who openly shared their challenges, hopes, and day-to-day realities. Your honesty and real-world experiences shaped the heart of this book and gave purpose to every page.

To Mr. Abhinav Agarwal and the Pendown Press Team

Thank you for your patience, attention, and care in shaping this book. Your support helped bring these thoughts to life in the best possible way.

And to my friends, well-wishers, and extended family, whether mentioned here or not, your encouragement has always mattered.

This book is the result of many hands and many hearts.

For all the support and belief, I am sincerely grateful.

Know Your Author

Entrepreneurship, when done honestly, is not built on ideas. It is built on execution, failure, correction, and repetition.

Sumeet Katariya's journey began long before software, startups, or elevator systems. Raised in a middle-class family in Ahilyanagar, Maharashtra, he learned business not from textbooks, but by observing customers at his father's shop, studying buying behaviour, understanding hesitation, and earning trust. When financial responsibility arrived early, at the age of 11, selling was no longer a skill. It became survival.

That early exposure shaped a mindset rooted in execution, discipline, and respect for real business struggle.

After completing his engineering education and experiencing corporate work firsthand, Sumeet chose the harder path of building something of his own. In 2016, Accucia Softwares was started from a small 1BHK setup, with no external funding and no safety net. What followed was not overnight success, but years of relentless building, selling, failing, fixing, and repeating.

Building Products from the Ground Up

In the early phase of India's GST rollout, when confusion and resistance were widespread among small businesses, Sumeet built and scaled BillPanda, an all-in-one billing platform tailored specifically for Indian MSMEs. BillPanda was designed to work offline, recognising the infrastructure realities of small towns and retail shops.

The platform covered:

- GST billing and compliance
- Inventory and stock management
- Sales, purchase, and material tracking
- Ledgers and basic accounting
- Third-party integrations for operational continuity

More importantly, BillPanda was not deployed remotely.

Sumeet personally implemented the system across 600+ retail shops and businesses across Maharashtra, sitting with shop owners, understanding resistance, training staff, and solving real-time issues.

That phase gave him something few product builders gain early, first-hand understanding of MSME pain points, technology adoption barriers, and the importance of simplicity over sophistication. It taught him how user-friendly design directly affects business discipline and quality of life for business owners.

Scaling Platforms, Not Just Products

As Accucia Softwares evolved, Sumeet led the acquisition of AdBanao in collaboration with his business partner, transforming it into a scalable business promotion platform used across India. Under his leadership, AdBanao grew into a nationally recognised solution, today serving over 50 lakh users.

This phase reinforced another core principle.

Products scale only when they are people-driven, intuitive, and aligned with how businesses actually operate.

Across his journey, Accucia delivered 730+ custom digital transformation projects, including mobile applications, workflow systems, and CRM platforms across multiple industries. Sumeet worked with enterprises and institutions alike, but his focus remained rooted in solving real operational problems, not chasing vanity metrics.

From MSMEs to the Elevator Industry

Sumeet's deep involvement with MSMEs naturally led him into the elevator industry, one of the most operationally complex and long-term responsibility-driven sectors.

Working closely with elevator manufacturers, traders, and service providers, he observed a familiar pattern. Capable businesses were struggling not due to demand or skill, but because operations were fragmented, manual, and people-dependent.

Applying everything he had learned from BillPanda to AdBanao, Sumeet took an on-ground, observation-first approach. He studied elevator workflows, service realities, AMC economics, compliance pressure, and technician coordination in real environments.

That journey led to ElevatorPlus, a platform designed not as software, but as an operational system that fits how elevator businesses actually run.

Today, ElevatorPlus is used by elevator businesses across India and globally, helping owners regain control, reduce stress, and scale without operational chaos.

In this book, Sumeet shares insights drawn from real business situations, helping global elevator leaders rethink operations as a growth enabler, not a daily struggle.

His work is driven by a simple belief.

Businesses should grow with clarity, not chaos.

GrowthNiti, Thinking Beyond Software

Beyond products, Sumeet shares hard-earned insights through GrowthNiti, a platform focused on real business thinking.

GrowthNiti is not about motivation.

It is about clarity.

Here, Sumeet speaks openly about:

- Business growth rooted in systems
- Operational discipline over hustle
- Authority built through execution
- Lessons learned from real failures and scale

For founders who want to grow without noise, shortcuts, or chaos, GrowthNiti offers something rare, experience without filters.

Scan the **QR code** to stay connected with Sumeet and continue the thinking beyond this book.

For more info, Visit:

www.sumeetkatariya.info

Sumeet Katariya

Founder, Accucia Softwares Pvt. Ltd. | Creator of ElevatorPlus

Founder's Note

A Message from Sumeet (Accucia Softwares)

Over the years, while working closely with elevator businesses across sizes and regions, one thing became very clear to us:

Most elevator businesses are not struggling because they lack capability, they struggle because their operations are scattered.

We saw business owners personally tracking service calls.

We saw teams depending on memory instead of systems.

We saw growth slowing down not due to lack of orders, but due to lack of control.

ElevatorPlus was not created as "another software."

It was created as a **response to repeated, on-ground industry pain.**

This book is our attempt to share that understanding, not as a technical document, but as a business conversation.

If it helps you reduce stress, gain clarity, or rethink how you run operations, it has done its job.

CHAPTER 1

The Silent Backbone of Modern Life — Elevators in Our Daily World

"An elevator is trusted thousands of times before it is ever questioned once."

Most of us barely think about elevators.

We step in, press a button, glance at our phones, and step out a few seconds later. When everything works, elevators fade into the background of daily life. They do their job quietly, efficiently, without asking for attention.

It is only when an elevator stops working that we suddenly notice how important it really is.

Yet, every day, millions of people depend on elevators, in residential towers, hospitals, offices, malls, factories, and transport hubs. In many ways, elevators are not just machines; they are **critical infrastructure** that keeps modern life moving vertically.

For building owners, the perspective shifts slightly. Elevators are about reliability, compliance, and long-term value. A well-maintained elevator protects the building's reputation, reduces complaints, and meets regulatory requirements. It is an asset that reflects how responsibly a property is managed.

Facility managers see elevators through yet another lens. For them, it is about uptime, response time, coordination, and accountability. One breakdown can disrupt dozens or hundreds of people. Every delay becomes a phone call, a message, or a complaint that needs handling.

But for elevator manufacturers, traders, and service providers, elevators represent something deeper and far more complex.

They are not one-time products. They are living systems.

An elevator involves design decisions, site conditions, installation quality, spare parts, service teams, preventive maintenance, documentation, inspections, and ongoing support. Every installation marks the beginning of a long relationship, not the end of a sale. That relationship can last twenty, thirty, or even forty years.

Unlike many products that are sold once and forgotten, elevators stay with the customer for decades.

Every installation creates a long-term relationship, with expectations that grow year after year.

This makes the elevator business unique.

Growth is not only about selling more units. It is about managing what you sell, day after day, year after year, without stress or chaos.

As cities grow taller and buildings become smarter, elevators are no longer optional conveniences. They are mission-critical systems. And with that importance comes responsibility: operational, financial, and reputational.

This book is written for those who operate behind the scenes. The people who plan, manage, service, respond, and solve problems quietly. The ones who make sure that this silent backbone of modern life never breaks.

CHAPTER 2

Where the Elevator Industry Is Really Growing

The elevator industry is not just growing; it is evolving.

The elevator industry is definitely growing, but more importantly, it is changing its shape.

For years, growth was mostly measured by new installations. More buildings meant more elevators, and more elevators meant more business. Urbanisation, vertical housing, commercial complexes, hospitals, metros, airports, and smart city projects continue to push demand upward. That part of the story is visible and easy to understand.

But if you look a little deeper, you will notice that the real growth of the industry is happening somewhere else.

New installations may open the door, but long-term value is being created after the elevator is already running.

Today, the industry is expanding in **three powerful directions:**

1. Service & Maintenance Expansion

Every elevator that gets installed immediately creates a long-term responsibility. Annual Maintenance Contracts (AMC), routine servicing, emergency breakdown calls, part replacements, upgrades, and modernization all follow. For many companies, this recurring work now contributes a larger share of revenue than new sales.

This is what makes the elevator business unusually stable. Elevators do not disappear after installation. They stay in use for decades. If service operations are handled properly, this recurring nature can support predictable income and long-term relationships. But if it is handled poorly, it can quickly become a source of stress, complaints, and financial strain.

2. Compliance & Safety Expectations

Regulations, audits, safety certifications, and documentation requirements are increasing. Customers are more informed, authorities are stricter, and accountability is higher.

Growth now depends on how reliably you can meet safety standards, not just how fast you can install a lift.

3. Organised & System-Driven Players

Globally and locally, organised elevator businesses are gaining ground. What differentiates them is not always product superiority; it is operational control.

They know:

- Where their assets are
- Which elevators need attention
- Which customers are profitable and which ones are draining resources
- Where time, money, and efforts are being wasted

This clarity allows them to scale faster, serve better, and stress less.

The industry is no longer forgiving of chaos.

Growth is now rewarding those who can **execute consistently.**

"Growth without operational maturity increases liability faster than revenue."

CHAPTER 3

What Truly Gives Exponential Growth to an Elevator Business

"Growth does not fail because of ambition. It fails because responsibility grows faster than control."

Most elevator businesses believe that growth is mainly about effort.

More sales calls.

More technicians.

More installations.

More territory.

All of these actions do contribute to growth, especially in the early stages. But they do not create exponential growth.

Exponential growth in the elevator industry does not come from doing more.

It comes **from doing the same things better, faster, and with less friction.**

In the early phase of a business, effort often fills the gaps left by missing systems. Owners personally track installations and payment follow-ups. Senior staff step in whenever there is a service escalation. Inventory is managed through experience, memory, and quick phone calls. Everyone knows what is going on because the scale is still manageable.

This approach works for a while. The problem begins when scale arrives.

As the number of installed elevators increases, complexity does not grow in a straight line. It multiplies.

Every new installation adds years of service responsibility.

Every AMC brings recurring commitments that do not pause.

Every new technician adds another layer of coordination, scheduling, and supervision.

More work leads to more delays.

More people lead to more miscommunication.

More customers lead to more complaints.

This is where many elevator businesses feel stuck. Sales may still be happening, but growth starts to feel heavy instead of exciting.

True exponential growth only begins when operations are structured in a way that reduces dependence on individual effort.

- ➢ Execution becomes repeatable, not improvised
- ➢ Information becomes accessible, not hidden in someone's head
- ➢ Decisions become predictable, not reactive.
- ➢ The business runs on clarity, not heroics

When operations are structured, every action compounds:

- ➢ Faster installations improve cash cycles
- ➢ Timely service improves customer lifetime value
- ➢ Accurate records improve compliance and trust

In such businesses, growth does not feel aggressive.

It feels **controlled.** The organisation expands, but stress does not rise at the same speed.

Consider two elevator businesses with similar sales:

- One struggles with delayed installations, missed service calls, inventory confusion, and unhappy customers.
- The other delivers on time, tracks everything, resolves issues faster, and retains customers effortlessly.

The difference is not ambition. The difference is operational maturity.

"Growth in the elevator industry is cumulative obligation growth, not linear sales growth."

CHAPTER 4

The Current Reality — When Operations Become the Biggest Growth Bottleneck

> *"When growth outpaces systems, operations quietly become the problem."*

In most elevator businesses today, operations have grown faster than systems.

What once worked with 10 elevators begins to fail at 50.

What worked with 2 technicians collapses at 15.

What was manageable in one city becomes chaotic across locations.

On the outside, the business looks active. Phones keep ringing. Teams are constantly moving. Work is getting done. But underneath, control is slowly slipping away.

This is not because people are careless or irresponsible. It happens because the business has outgrown the way it operates.

The Reality on the Ground

Let us look at situations that will feel familiar to almost anyone in the elevator industry:

- A service call comes in, but no one knows which technician is free
- Spare parts are ordered, but inventory data is outdated
- AMC renewals are missed, simply because reminders don't exist
- Installation schedules shift, but teams are not aligned
- Compliance documents are stored, but not easily retrievable

None of this happens due to negligence.

It happens because manual coordination has limits.

Most small and mid-sized elevator businesses still rely on a mix of tools that were never meant to handle scale. WhatsApp groups are used to coordinate teams. Excel sheets track installations and service visits. Phone calls handle urgent escalations. Critical knowledge lives in individual heads. When something is unclear, the solution is often, "Ask him, he knows."

This approach works when the business is small and everyone is closely involved. But as volume increases, cracks begin to show. Information gets scattered. Updates are missed. Decisions are made based on partial visibility.

At a certain scale, operations stop supporting growth and start blocking it.

Business owners feel busy all day, yet end the day unsure if things are actually under control. There is activity everywhere, but clarity nowhere. Problems keep getting solved, but the same problems keep returning.

This is the moment when operations quietly turn into a bottleneck.

At this point, sales no longer solve problems.

Hiring no longer fixes delays.

Effort only increases stress.

The business reaches a ceiling, not because of the market, but because operations cannot carry the load.

Recognizing this moment is critical. Because beyond it, growth without structure becomes dangerous.

From Daily Firefighting to Knowing What's Actually Happening

"We were busy all day, but nothing felt under control. Service calls were coming in, technicians were on the move, and inventory was being purchased, yet decisions were still based on calls and memory.

Operations were spread across WhatsApp, Excel, and people's heads. Growth was happening, but clarity was missing.

Reading this chapter felt like someone had described our daily reality word for word."

~Owner, Elevator Installation & Service Company | India

CHAPTER 5

The Real Cost of Operational Bottlenecks on Business Growth

"Operational bottlenecks don't announce themselves. They leak value silently."

What These Bottlenecks Really Cost You

Because the damage is gradual, it often goes unnoticed. The business may still look busy. Revenue may still be coming in. Teams may still be working long hours. Yet beneath the surface, small gaps begin to add up.

The real cost of operational bottlenecks is not always visible on a balance sheet. But it is felt everywhere.

1. Lost Revenue (Without You Realising)

AMC renewals are missed because no reminder system exists. Billing after installations gets delayed because paperwork is incomplete or scattered. Service visits happen, but records are not properly updated, making it difficult to bill accurately or justify charges later.

None of this happens in one large incident. Money does not disappear overnight. It leaks slowly, in small amounts, across days and months. By the time the loss becomes visible, it feels normal, almost accepted.

2. Customer Trust Erosion

Most customers are reasonable. A delayed response once in a while is understandable. Even a mistake can be forgiven if handled well. But inconsistency changes perception.

When follow-ups are missed repeatedly or responses keep getting delayed, customers begin to form quiet opinions. They may say things like, “They are good, but not organised,” or “We have to follow up too much.” Eventually, the thought arises, “Let’s explore other options next time.”

Trust does not usually break when a contract ends. It breaks much earlier, quietly, while the relationship still appears intact.

3. Team Burnout & Dependency

When systems don't exist, people fill the gaps. Owners become the system. Senior staff become decision points for everything. Junior team members wait for instructions instead of acting confidently.

This creates pressure at the top and hesitation at the bottom. Growth then depends on who is available rather than what the business is capable of handling. When key people are absent, everything slows down.

4. Mental Load on the Business Owner

Owners carry a running list in their head all day. Pending service calls. Missed follow-ups. Inventory that may or may not be available. Complaints that might arrive. Problems that could surface without warning.

This constant background thinking drains energy. It reduces the space needed for strategic decisions. The business may be growing on paper, but the owner feels stuck, overwhelmed, and unable to step back.

Operational inefficiency doesn't just reduce profit; it steals peace of mind.

CHAPTER 6

Why ElevatorPlus Was Born

> *"ElevatorPlus was not born from an idea. It was born from repetition."*

Across different cities, different company sizes, and different business models, the same operational issues appeared again and again. The people were different, the locations were different, but the issues were almost identical. It became hard to ignore the pattern.

Elevator businesses were capable.

Their teams were hardworking.

Their demand was strong.

Yet growth remained fragile. A small disruption could throw things off balance. Owners felt they were constantly managing problems rather than building the business.

The common thread was clear: operations had grown organically, but without structure.

Generic software solutions did not help either. They treated elevator companies like just another service business. They failed to understand what makes this industry different. Elevators are not one-time jobs. They involve long-term service commitments. AMC structures are layered and sensitive. Compliance is not optional. Technician work happens in real buildings, under real constraints, not inside a neat office workflow.

Accucia chose to step back and look at the elevator business as it actually operates.

Instead of adapting generic systems, the focus shifted to understanding the elevator business deeply:

- How installations transition into service
- How breakdowns impact trust
- How AMC leakages affect profitability
- How documentation protects reputation
- How owners carry hidden operational load

ElevatorPlus was built around these questions.

It was not designed as a collection of features. It was designed as an operational framework that mirrors the real flow of an elevator business. From installation to service. From breakdown to resolution. From contract to compliance. From daily coordination to long-term visibility.

The goal was not automation for the sake of technology. The goal was control without complexity.

ElevatorPlus exists to replace chaos with clarity, dependency with systems, and stress with predictability.

Most importantly, it was built to support growth in a healthy way, not just enable expansion.

Why We Stopped Using Five Tools and Still Had No Control

"Before ElevatorPlus, we used one system for attendance, another for technician tracking, Excel for AMC, and WhatsApp for coordination. Despite spending money on multiple tools, nothing was connected.

We still depended on manual follow-ups and senior staff to hold things together.

ElevatorPlus was the first system that actually understood how our elevator operations work, not as isolated tasks, but as one flow."

~Director, Elevator Trading & Maintenance Company | Middle East

CHAPTER 7

The 5 Biggest Elevator Industry Challenges and Why They Persist

"The problem is not that these challenges exist. The problem is that they repeat."

Every elevator business faces challenges. That part is expected.

What's surprising is not that these challenges exist, but how similar they are across businesses, regardless of size or geography.

Over the years of industry interaction, five challenges appear repeatedly.

Challenge 1: Spares & Inventory Chaos

Most elevator businesses don't suffer from lack of spares;

they suffer from lack of visibility.

- ➢ Spares exist, but no one knows exact stock
- ➢ Wrong parts are sent to site
- ➢ Emergency purchases happen despite inventory lying unused
- ➢ Capital remains blocked without clarity

This leads to higher costs, delays, and frustration, all caused by disconnected inventory management.

Challenge 2: Inefficient Breakdown & Service Call Handling

A breakdown is not just a technical event; it's an operational test.

Common issues include:

- ➢ Calls logged manually
- ➢ Technician allocation based on availability guesswork
- ➢ No service history available at site
- ➢ Delayed closures due to poor coordination

What should be a calm, controlled process often turns into reactive firefighting. The problem is not the breakdown, but how the response is managed.

Challenge 3: AMC & Preventive Maintenance Leakages

AMC is meant to be stable, predictable revenue. Yet, many elevator businesses experience:

- Missed renewals
- Incomplete preventive maintenance records
- No visibility into contract status
- Poor follow-up discipline

Revenue exists on paper, but realisation suffers due to weak tracking.

Challenge 4: Compliance, Documentation & Audit Stress

Elevator businesses deal with:

- Safety certificates
- Inspection reports
- Government compliance
- Customer documentation

When documents are scattered:

- Audits become stressful
- Information retrieval is slow
- Risk exposure increases

Compliance should build confidence, not anxiety.

Challenge 5: People Dependency Instead of System Dependence

In many businesses:

- One person "knows everything"
- One senior handles all escalations
- Knowledge is not documented, only remembered

This makes growth fragile. When people leave or are unavailable, operations slow down or break completely.

Scalable businesses depend on systems, not individuals.

These five challenges are not isolated problems. They are connected. They all point to one root cause:

Operations that have grown without structure.

Until that changes, these challenges will continue to repeat, no matter how much effort or experience a business has.

CHAPTER 8

Why Smoother Operations Are the Key to 3X Growth in Elevator Business

"Demand was never the problem. Handling it was."

In the elevator industry, lack of demand is rarely the real problem. Buildings are rising, equipment is ageing, and service needs never stop. What holds businesses back is something far less visible. Growth fails when operations cannot handle it smoothly.

When operations are rough, every new order adds pressure. Every new customer increases stress. Growth begins to feel risky rather than exciting. But when operations become smooth, the effect is surprisingly powerful. Small improvements start to multiply results.

The first impact shows up in execution and cash flow.

When installations, service calls, and billing are properly aligned, work closes faster. Technicians finish jobs with fewer delays. Paperwork does not wait in someone's inbox. Invoices go out on time, and payments follow more naturally. Cash flow improves without pushing the sales team harder or offering discounts. The same work simply converts into money more efficiently.

The second impact is on service quality and long-term revenue.

Customers rarely leave because of one mistake. They leave when the experience feels unreliable. Missed updates, delayed visits, and unclear communication slowly wear down trust. Smooth operations reduce these gaps. Service happens on time. Communication is clear. Records are accurate and easy to access.

This consistency strengthens customer relationships. AMC renewals become easier. Preventive maintenance stays on track. Referrals increase because customers feel confident recommending a business that feels dependable.

The third impact is on team performance.

When roles are clear and processes are defined, teams work better without working harder. Technicians focus on fixing problems, not figuring out what they are supposed to do next. Managers stop chasing updates across calls and messages. Information is available when needed.

As a result, owners stop micromanaging daily tasks. They no longer need to step in constantly to resolve confusion. Efficiency improves, and stress reduces across the organisation.

The biggest shift happens at the owner level.

With operational clarity, owners move out of daily firefighting. Instead of scanning WhatsApp messages and missed calls, they review clear reports. Decisions are based on facts rather than assumptions. Planning becomes possible because the business feels predictable.

This is where three times growth starts to feel realistic. Not as a bold claim, but as a natural outcome of better control. The business can take on more work without everything becoming heavier.

Smooth operations do not make noise. They do not attract attention. But they quietly multiply results.

Growth Without Increasing Daily Stress

"Our business did not grow because we hired more people or worked longer hours. It grew because operations became smoother.

Service response improved. AMC tracking became predictable. Inventory decisions stopped being reactive.

For the first time, growth felt manageable instead of exhausting."

~Managing Partner, Elevator Service Company | India

CHAPTER 9

How the World Is Growing Faster with Better Operational Control

"Hard work builds momentum. Control decides how far it goes."

Globally, industries are moving in one clear direction:

From effort-driven businesses to control-driven businesses

This shift is visible across manufacturing, logistics, healthcare, infrastructure, and elevators are no exception.

What Global Elevator Leaders Do Differently

- They track every asset
- They document every service action
- They monitor performance indicators
- They reduce dependency on memory

Growth is no longer dependent on "experience alone", it is supported by structured information.

Control Enables Scale Without Chaos

When operational control exists:

- New locations can be added smoothly
- Teams can expand without confusion
- Quality remains consistent

This is why global players scale faster while maintaining reliability. Their growth does not feel rushed. It feels planned.

The Lesson for Elevator Businesses

The future does not belong to those who work the hardest.

It belongs to those who control operations intelligently.

Technology alone does not solve problems.

But technology aligned with industry reality does.

This is where purpose-built operational systems begin to matter.

"We Thought an Indian System Wouldn't Fit Our Operations"

"Our initial hesitation was simple: we assumed an Indian-built system would not align with our local processes and regulations. Distance was another concern.

What surprised us was how smoothly ElevatorPlus adapted to our operational structure. The onboarding was structured, remote implementation was clear, and support never felt distant.

It did not feel like using software from another country. It felt like using a system that understood elevator operations universally."

~Managing Director, Elevator Service & Modernization Company | Europe

CHAPTER 10

The Right Trust Matrix for Sustainable Elevator Businesses: Operations × Utility × Brand × Longevity

"Trust grows from experience, not promises."

In the elevator business, trust is not created by promises or presentations.

It is created by **consistent experience over time.**

Customers may choose you for price or relationships initially,

but they stay with you only when trust deepens.

That trust is built on a four-part matrix.

1. Operations: The Foundation of Trust

Operations are what customers experience daily.

- Did the technician arrive on time?
- Was the issue resolved properly?
- Was communication clear?
- Was the documentation accurate?

Even the strongest brand fails if operations are weak.

Operations are invisible when done right, and impossible to hide when done wrong.

2. Utility: How Useful You Are After the Sale

Elevator businesses are not judged only at installation.

They are judged:

- During breakdowns
- During emergencies
- During audits
- During renewals

Utility means being useful when it matters most.

Smooth operations ensure:

- Faster response
- Better service history
- More informed decisions at the site

Utility increases when information is available, not scattered.

The more useful you are after the sale, the stronger the trust becomes.

3. Brand: The Outcome of Repeated Experience

In the elevator industry, brand is not advertising.

Brand is what customers say when:

- You are not in the room
- A new project is discussed
- A recommendation is asked for

A strong brand is built quietly, through reliability, discipline, and control.

Operational maturity strengthens brand credibility automatically.

4. Longevity: The Real Goal of Elevator Businesses

Elevator businesses are built for decades, not quarters.

Longevity depends on:

- Stable revenue
- Retained customers
- Reduced dependency on individuals
- Scalable systems

Businesses that survive generations are not the busiest ones,

they are the most structured ones.

When operations, utility, brand, and longevity align, trust becomes automatic. It no longer depends on personal follow-ups or constant reassurance. It becomes part of how the business functions.

When Customers Started Trusting the Process, Not Just People

"Earlier, customers trusted us because of relationships. Today, they trust us because our process is clear.

Service records, preventive maintenance, and documentation are consistent. There is less confusion and fewer follow-ups.

ElevatorPlus helped us build operational trust, which directly strengthened our brand."

~Owner, Elevator Manufacturing & AMC Company | Europe

CHAPTER 11

How This Operational Shift Will Shape the Future of the Elevator Industry

"The way we work today decides where we stand tomorrow."

The elevator industry is slowly approaching a clear divide. It may not be obvious at first glance, but it is already forming.

On one side:

- Reactive businesses
- Manual coordination
- Firefighting-driven growth

On the other:

- Predictive businesses
- System-driven operations
- Calm, controlled scaling

This divide will define the future of the industry.

What the Future Elevator Business Will Look Like

The elevator business of tomorrow will look very different from what many are used to today. Every elevator will have a clear and complete service history that anyone authorised can access. There will be no guessing about what was done last month or last year. Every AMC will be trackable, with renewals, visits, and obligations clearly visible. Every technician's work will be recorded, not to control people, but to support better planning and accountability. And every major decision will be supported by real information, not assumptions or last-minute calls.

This shift is not optional. It is already happening.

Customers Will Demand More Transparency

As buildings become more complex and expectations rise, customers are changing too. Building owners, RWAs, and facility managers are far more informed than they were earlier. They ask sharper questions. They expect clear timelines, proper documentation, and reliable reporting. They want to know what work was done, when it was done, and what comes next.

Operational opacity will no longer be accepted as normal. "We will check and get back" is slowly losing its place. Transparency is becoming a basic expectation, not a premium offering.

This change puts pressure on elevator businesses, but it also creates opportunity.

Businesses That Adapt Will Lead

Those who embrace operational clarity early will:

- Win larger projects
- Handle scale without stress
- Build stronger partnerships

The future elevator industry will reward control, not chaos.

CHAPTER 12

Why Accucia Softwares Chose This Path

Accucia Softwares did not start with a product idea.

It started with a problem of obsession.

Why More Tools Didn't Mean Better Operations

Across many elevator businesses, technology was already present, but in pieces.

WhatsApp was used for daily coordination.
Excel sheets tracked jobs and follow-ups.
One tool handled attendance and payroll.
Another tracked technician location.
Another managed inventory.
Yet another handled AMC reminders.

Each tool solved a small, isolated problem.
Together, they created fragmentation.
Data remained scattered across platforms.
Teams repeated the same work in different places.
Owners still relied on calls, memory, and personal intervention to connect information.

Despite spending on multiple tools, there was no single, reliable view of operations, no clear understanding of what was happening, what was delayed, or where inefficiencies were building. The tools existed, but outcomes did not improve.

Across interactions with elevator businesses, one pattern was consistent:

The industry did not need generic software. It needed industry-aware operational intelligence.

Why Generic Tools Fail Elevator Businesses

Most generic systems:

- Are not designed for elevator workflows
- Ignore AMC and service realities
- Add complexity instead of removing it

Accucia chose to go deeper, not wider.

Choosing Specialisation Over Scale

Rather than building for everyone, Accucia focused on:

- Elevator manufacturers
- Elevator traders
- Elevator service providers

This focus allowed real-world alignment with:

- Installation cycles
- Breakdown workflows
- Compliance structures
- Inventory realities

The decision was clear:

Build something that fits the elevator business as it is. Do not force elevator businesses to fit into generic software designed for something else.

That is the path Accucia Softwares chose. Not the easiest one. Not the fastest one. But the one that could actually make operations clearer, calmer, and more dependable for an industry that runs on long term trust and responsibility.

Build something that fits the elevator business, not force elevator businesses to fit software.

CHAPTER 13

How Accucia Resolves Operational Challenges Through ElevatorPlus

"Clarity is the strongest operational advantage."

ElevatorPlus was designed with one principle:

Clarity should replace chaos.

Most elevator businesses are already working hard. Teams are busy. Tools are in place. Data exists somewhere. The real problem is that everything lives in separate pockets. Information moves slowly. Decisions depend on follow ups. Owners step in not because they want to, but because they have to.

ElevatorPlus does not try to add another layer of work. It connects what already exists and brings it into one clear flow.

What ElevatorPlus Changes at the Core

- Information moves faster than people
- Decisions are supported by visibility
- Teams operate with confidence
- Owners regain control without micromanaging

Operations become predictable, and predictability enables growth.

From Fragmented to Unified Operations

One of the biggest changes ElevatorPlus brings is moving businesses from fragmented operations to unified ones.

Service management, AMC tracking, inventory visibility, documentation control, and team coordination are no longer treated as separate activities. They work together as one connected system. A service call links to the elevator history. AMC details connect to preventive maintenance. Inventory usage reflects real service activity. Documentation stays attached to the job where it belongs.

This unified approach removes duplication and confusion. Teams stop updating the same information in multiple places. Follow ups reduce. Errors drop. Everyone works from the same source of truth.

The Result: Calm, Scalable Growth

Businesses using structured operations experience:

- Reduced stress
- Better customer retention
- Faster response times
- Stronger leadership clarity

Growth stops feeling heavy, and starts feeling manageable.

Not Another Software, A System That Fits Elevator Businesses

"What makes ElevatorPlus different is not features. It is understanding.

It fits how elevator businesses actually operate: installations, breakdowns, AMC, inventory, compliance, all connected.

This is not a tool we log into. It is a system we now rely on."

~CEO, Elevator Solutions Company | Southeast Asia

Security, Compliance, and Scale, Without Compromise

"Before implementation, our main concerns were data security, compliance with local regulations, and whether the system could scale as our operations grew.

ElevatorPlus addressed these clearly. Data controls were defined, access was structured, and compliance requirements were accommodated without friction.

The flexibility to adapt to country-specific changes while remaining stable at scale gave us long-term confidence in the system."

~CEO, Elevator Operations Company | Middle East

CHAPTER 14

If I Were Starting an Elevator Company Again Today

"Growth becomes easier when memory is replaced by systems."

If I were starting an elevator company again today, I would do many things differently, not because the market has changed, but because my understanding of what actually limits growth has matured.

The first thing I would stop doing immediately is confusing activity with progress.

I would not run follow-ups manually.

I would not depend on WhatsApp groups to move work forward.

I would not allow Excel sheets to become the backbone of operations.

And I would never again build a business that runs on a few "heroes" who keep everything in their head.

Hero-dependence feels efficient in the beginning. It looks like control.

In reality, it is a silent risk.

When one person knows where the AMC data is, one person knows which technician is free, and one person remembers which quotation needs follow-up, the business is not scaling. It is balancing on memory. And memory always breaks before the business is ready.

"If I were starting again, my first investment would not be sales, marketing, or hiring. It would be structure."

From **Day 1**, I would implement a single source of truth.

One system where leads, quotations, installations, AMCs, breakdowns, inventory, payments, and people data live together. Not connected loosely. Not synced once a week. One place. Always current. Always trusted.

I would build role-based dashboards from the start.

Not reports made for review meetings, but dashboards made for daily decisions.

- A founder dashboard that shows reality, not optimism
- A service dashboard that shows what is pending, not what was promised
- A technician view that shows only what matters to execute the job

People don't fail because they are careless. They fail because they don't see the full picture.

I would enforce zero memory-based operations.

If something is important, it must exist in the system.

If it is not in the system, it does not exist.

No “I will remember.”

No “ask him, he knows.”

No “it’s written somewhere.”

Memory does not scale. Systems do.

Most importantly, I would systemise early, not “after we grow”.

Because here is the truth most founders learn late:

Early systemisation compounds faster than sales or hiring.

Sales gives you volume.

Hiring gives you capacity.

Systems give you leverage.

With systems in place:

- Each new lead is handled better than the last
- Each new technician becomes productive faster
- Each new AMC reduces chaos instead of adding to it

Without systems, growth multiplies confusion.

With systems, growth multiplies clarity.

If I were starting again today, my goal would not be to look busy.

It would be to build a business that runs without me needing to remember, chase, or intervene daily.

Because real freedom in business does not come from working harder.

It comes from designing the business so it does not depend on you to survive.

That is the difference between running an elevator company and building one that actually scales.

"The biggest regret in business is not making a wrong decision. It's delaying the right one. And the right time to build systems is always earlier than you think."

Appendix A
When NOT to Systemise Yet

There is a dangerous assumption in business today: that systems automatically solve problems.

They don't.

Systems amplify reality.

If reality is unclear, systems only make confusion faster.

Over the years, we have seen elevator businesses fail not because they delayed systemisation, but because they implemented systems at the wrong time.

Here are situations where pausing is the wiser decision.

1. When Roles Are Undefined

If responsibilities live in people's heads and overlap constantly, no system will fix that.

Software cannot decide who owns what.

Clarity must come first.

2. When the Business Runs on Exceptions, Not Processes

If every installation, service call, or AMC is handled "case by case," systemisation will feel restrictive and frustrating.

Systems work best when 80% of work follows repeatable patterns.

3. When Leadership Is Avoiding Visibility

Some founders delay systems because they don't want uncomfortable truths exposed, such as delayed billing, poor follow-ups, or weak margins.

Systems don't create problems.

They reveal them.

4. When Discipline Is Missing

A system only works when data is entered honestly and consistently.

If the culture is "we'll update later," no technology will help.

5. When the Expectation Is Instant ROI

Systems are not vending machines.

They don't deliver outcomes the moment you log in.

They deliver predictability first, and results later.

The right time to systemise is not when things are breaking, but when you are ready to see the business as it truly is.

Appendix B
Operational Maturity Checklist for Elevator Businesses

This is not a readiness test.

It is a self-reflection tool.

Answer honestly.

Leadership & Visibility

- Do you know, today, how many service calls are pending, without asking anyone?
- Can you see AMC renewals due in the next 30–60 days without reminders?
- Can decisions be made without WhatsApp screenshots?

Service & Maintenance

- Is service history available before sending a technician?
- Are preventive maintenance visits tracked, not assumed?
- Are repeat complaints visible as patterns, not anecdotes?

Installations & Projects

- Can you see installation progress without calling the site?
- Are delays visible early, or only when customers escalate?
- Is billing linked to actual project milestones?

Inventory & Spares

- Do you know what stock exists before making emergency purchases?
- Can you trace which spare went to which site?
- Is capital blocked in inventory visible, not guessed?

People & Dependency

- Can operations continue smoothly if one senior person is unavailable?
- Is knowledge documented or remembered?
- Do technicians know their daily priorities without chasing instructions?

Documentation & Compliance

- Are certificates, reports, and approvals retrievable in minutes?
- Are audits stressful or routine?
- Is compliance proactive or reactive?

Founder Load

- Are you solving strategic problems, or operational follow-ups?
- Does the business move when you step away for a day?
- Is growth increasing clarity, or pressure?

If most answers create discomfort, that is not failure. It is awareness.

And awareness is the first step toward maturity.

Epilogue
The Calm, Controlled, Scalable Elevator Business

The elevator business does not need more effort.

It needs better structure.

For years, growth in this industry has been mistaken for busyness. Long days, constant calls, and daily firefighting are often worn as badges of honour. But stress is not a sign of success, and chaos is not a growth strategy. They are signals that the business is carrying more responsibility than its structure can support.

Calm growth looks different. It is quieter. Work moves forward without constant follow-ups. Teams know what to do without being chased. Decisions are made with clarity, not urgency. Customers feel the difference, even if they cannot always name it.

Businesses that grow calmly:

- Last longer
- Earn deeper trust
- Create stronger legacies

This book is not the end.

It is an invitation to rethink operations, regain control, and build an elevator business that grows without breaking the people running it.

The goal is simple. Build an elevator business that grows steadily, serves reliably, and does not break the people running it.

Because the strongest businesses are not the loudest ones. They are the most controlled.

A Personal Invitation

First of all, I would like to thank you for giving your valuable time to this book.

If you have reached this point in the book, one thing is clear:

you are thinking seriously about how your elevator business operates.

Not about tools.

Not about software.

About systems.

Over the years, we have worked closely with hundreds of elevator manufacturers, traders, and service companies, helping them move from manual, people-dependent operations to structured, predictable systems. In that process, we've learned one important truth:

Not every business is ready to implement systems, and that's okay.

Before technology, there must be clarity.

In our experience, many business owners get distracted at this stage.

Some start looking at large players in the industry and try to copy their systems, without considering whether those systems fit their own scale, team structure, or maturity level. Others invest in solutions simply because a competitor is using them, not because they have clarity on what problem they are actually solving.

In some cases, a convincing salesperson presents a polished solution. The pitch sounds right, the demo looks impressive, and a decision is made quickly. Months later, the business is left with unused software, wasted money, and reduced trust in systems altogether.

This strategy call exists to protect you from that trap.

What This Call Is and What It Is Not

We invite you to a one-to-one virtual strategy call where we will:

- Review your current operational structure
- Identify where control is missing or leaking
- Help you understand whether systems will genuinely help your business today
- Guide you through the preliminary steps required before any implementation

This call is not a sales discussion.

There is no obligation, no pressure, and no commitment expected.

Why We Are Offering This

We have seen too many capable elevator businesses lose time, money, and confidence by adopting systems that were never right for them.

In our regular consulting practice, this 60-minute strategic review is valued at INR 24,999. For readers of this book, we are offering it completely free, as a genuine effort to help you make the right decision at the right time.

How to Schedule

Scan the QR code or use the link provided to book your strategy call at a time that works for you.

Come with honesty.

Leave with direction.

Or Visit: https://elevatorplus.app/demo-request

We look forward to connecting with you and understanding your journey better.

Whatever stage your business is at today, we wish you clarity, confidence, and steady growth ahead.

With Best Wishes,

Sumeet Katariya